THE SECRET LIFE OF FOOD

THE SECRET

LIFE OF FOOD

CLARE CRESPO

PHOTOGRAPHS BY **ERIC STAUDENMAIER**

A MELCHER MEDIA BOOK

HYPERION PAPERBACKS FOR CHILDREN
NEW YORK

FOR THE PANDAS

CONTENTS

PLANTS & INSECTS

ANATOMY

HOME

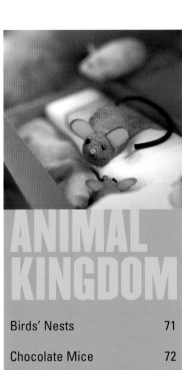

ANIMAL KINGDOM

SUMMER VACATION

MASTER RECIPES

When I was a kid, I imagined that hot dogs wrapped in bis

cheese was a nearby haystack for those piggies to play in.

and cookies became tiny canvases. I still have the mind of

a strange obsession, but I love being able to surprise and de

the shape of a pair of pants and a shirt to a party raises ent

piece? It all depends on how you look at it. For me, food is

I hope that these recipes will be an inspiration. Dor

are reading a recipe, be creative. Let your cooking tell tl

your pals to some Monkey Pops. Celebrate official holidays

mer —how about serving Hawaiian Shirt Punch with dinne

some Monster Head Potatoes for lunch? Keep your mind wi

whole life will feel bigger and more fantastic. Have fun ai

dough were real pigs, cozy in their blankets. Macaroni and

grew a little older, cakes became sculptural, and cupcakes

x-year-old when it comes to creating in the kitchen. Call it

t my friends with my latest work of art. Bringing a cake in

ining to a new level. Delicious dessert? Funny conversation

t supply.

e afraid to come up with your own food art pieces. When you

orld who you are. If you are into monkeys (like I am), treat

ell as ones you think up yourself. It's the first day of sum-

your little brother loves scary movies, why not whip up

pen. If your everyday activities are not so everyday, your

t well!—*Clare Crespo*

TARANTULA COOKIES   CANDY BUGS   CHERRY ROS

TS &

ECTS

TERPILLAR CAKE   PRETZEL BUTTERFLIES   CARROT CAKE   SPIDERWEB SOUP   MERINGUE MUSHROOMS   FLOWER POT CAKES

INGREDIENTS

2 cups all-purpose flour

1/2 teaspoon baking powder

1/2 teaspoon salt

1/8 teaspoon baking soda

10 tablespoons unsalted butter, softened

1/2 cup light brown sugar

1/4 cup granulated sugar

1 egg

1 teaspoon vanilla extract

2 tablespoons unsweetened cocoa powder

1 bag (8 ounces) thin, short pretzel sticks

1 large bag (11-1/2 ounces) milk chocolate chips

2 tablespoons vegetable oil

chocolate sprinkles

small red candies

METHOD

1. Preheat the oven to 350°.

2. In a medium mixing bowl, combine the flour, baking powder, salt, and baking soda. Set aside.

3. In a large mixing bowl, beat together the butter, brown sugar, and granulated sugar until light and fluffy. Add the egg and vanilla and beat until well blended.

4. Gradually add the flour mixture and cocoa powder. Beat to form a smooth dough.

5. Roll a tablespoon-sized ball of dough, and place it on a baking sheet. Arrange eight pretzel sticks around the ball like spokes on a wheel. Press the tips of the pretzel sticks firmly into the dough ball. Continue with the rest of the pretzels and dough.

6. Bake until the cookies start to brown around the edges, about 7–10 minutes.

7. Lift the cookies from the baking sheets with a spatula, and place on wire cooling racks. Let cool completely. Place the racks on sheets of aluminum foil or waxed paper.

8. In a double boiler (or the microwave), melt the chocolate chips with vegetable oil.

9. Pour the melted chocolate over each cookie. Coat with chocolate sprinkles. Press in two red candy eyes on the front of the head. Eeek!

The perfect Halloween cookie.

Makes approximately 25–30 cookies

DON'T LET THE HAIRY ARMS AND LEGS ALARM YOU. TARANTULA COOKIES MIGHT LOOK FRISKY, BUT THEY DON'T BITE.

TARANTULACOOKIES

CANDYBUGS

A WELCOME INFESTATION ON ANY DAY. WHEN THESE
IMAGINATIVE BUGS SWARM INTO YOUR HOUSE,
PUT AWAY THE FLYSWATTER AND BUG SPRAY. WITH LUCK,
ONE WILL FLY STRAIGHT INTO YOUR MOUTH.

CANDY INGREDIENTS

4	tablespoons evaporated milk
1/2	teaspoon vanilla extract
4-1/2	cups powdered sugar
	assorted small candies and mixed nuts

METHOD

1. In a large mixing bowl, gently mix together the evaporated milk, vanilla extract, and the powdered sugar, using a fork, until mixture is very thick.

2. Knead mixture with your hands until it is smooth and easy to handle.

3. Shape the dough into insect shapes and decorate with small candies or mixed nuts. You can press some candies directly into the dough, but use the Icing Glue if needed.

ICING GLUE INGREDIENTS

1/4	cup powdered sugar
1	teaspoon water

METHOD

Mix together in a small bowl until the consistency
is similar to that of a paste.

Makes about 30 bugs

CHERRY ROSES

CHERRY ROSES MAKE A LOVELY BOUQUET. WITH THEIR BRIGHT RED CENTERS, THESE ROSES ARE GOOD ENOUGH TO EAT.

INGREDIENTS

- 2 packages prepared pie crust dough (or homemade if you have the time)
- 2 cans (4 cups) pitted red cherries
- 3 tablespoons cornstarch
- 3/4 cup sugar
- 1 teaspoon lemon juice
- 1/2 teaspoon almond extract
- 1/4 teaspoon salt

METHOD

1. Preheat the oven to 450°. Grease muffin tin.

2. Spread out prepared pastry dough. Cut pastry into rounds, using a 2-1/2" round cookie cutter or a glass.

3. Place one pastry round on the bottom of each muffin cup. Fit five pastry rounds around the sides of the cup, overlapping the edges. Press the edges and the bottom together firmly.

4. With a fork, prick the bottom and sides of each pastry. Bake 8–10 minutes, or until light golden brown.

5. Carefully remove each pastry from the pan and cool on cooling racks.

6. Drain the cherries, reserving 1 cup of the liquid.

7. Put the cornstarch in a saucepan over medium heat.

8. Gradually stir in the reserved cherry liquid.

9. Mix well and bring to a rapid boil, stirring constantly.

10. When the mixture is clear, add the sugar.

11. Remove from heat and mix in the lemon juice, almond extract, and salt. Gradually blend in the cherries. Let cool.

12. Fill each pastry cup with the cherry filling.

These are nice to make for people instead of giving them real flowers.

Makes 6 roses

INGREDIENTS

10 Hostess Sno Balls

2 google eyes (or gum drops)

2 pipe cleaners in any color

5 pipe cleaners in another color

   peanut butter

METHOD

1. Place Sno Balls in the shape of an "S" on a tray or a rectangular piece of cardboard.

2. Cut the five pipe cleaners in half to make ten legs. Stick two pipe cleaners into every second Sno Ball.

3. Twist the two remaining pipe cleaners into spirals for the antennae, and insert these on top of the head of the caterpillar.

4. Press eyes onto the head. Use a little peanut butter as adhesive.

5. Cut a medium-sized wedge out of the front of the head for the caterpillar's mouth.

This must be the fastest, funniest cake you can make. It also travels very well; you can bring the ingredients to a friend's house and make it in about five minutes.

Serves 10

CATERPILLARCAKE

THE CATERPILLAR CAKE INCHES ALONG THE STREET, LOOKING FOR A FUN PARTY. WILL IT STOP AT YOUR HOUSE?

PRETZELBUTTERFLIES

ON STILL MORNINGS IN A FOREST, LOOK OUT FOR THE GRACEFUL PRETZEL BUTTERFLY WITH ITS BROWN, SALTY WINGS. SPOTTING ONE IS CONSIDERED GOOD LUCK.

INGREDIENTS

8   caramel candies

16 knot-shaped pretzels

16 small pretzel sticks

METHOD

1. Unwrap the caramels and roll each into a ball shape, using your hands.

2. Stick one knot-shaped pretzel into each side of the caramel for the wings.

3. Stick two pretzel sticks in the front of the caramel for the antennae.

Make a whole swarm of butterflies by using other kinds of pretzels (yogurt-dipped, different sizes) and a variety of wing positions.

Makes 8 butterflies

CARROTCAKE

THIS GIANT CARROT CAKE IS THE PRIZE OF THE AGRICULTURAL COMMUNITY. KEEP THE BUNNIES AWAY.

CAKE INGREDIENTS

3 cups all-purpose flour, sifted before measuring

3 teaspoons baking soda

3 teaspoons double-acting baking powder

3 teaspoons cinnamon

1-1/2 teaspoons salt

2 cups vegetable oil

3 cups sugar

6 eggs, beaten

1 cup chopped walnuts or pecans

4-1/2 cups grated carrots

Serves 20

METHOD

1. Preheat the oven to 325°. Grease and flour one 8" square pan and one 9" x 13" rectangular pan.

2. In a large mixing bowl, sift together the flour, baking soda, baking powder, cinnamon, and salt.

3. In a separate bowl, mix together the oil, sugar, and eggs, and add to flour mixture. Stir well.

4. Add the nuts and carrots, and blend well.

5. Pour into both pans and bake about 1 hour 25 minutes, or until a toothpick inserted into the center comes out clean. Remove the cakes from the pans after 5 minutes, and let cool on racks.

6. Cut the rectangular cake into a triangular or carrot shape. Cut the square cake into a carrot greens shape. Arrange on tray.

ICING INGREDIENTS

14 ounces cream cheese

7 tablespoons milk

7 cups confectioners sugar, sifted

3 teaspoons vanilla extract

orange (mix red and yellow) and green food coloring

METHOD

1. In a medium mixing bowl, blend together the cream cheese and milk until soft and fluffy.

2. Gradually beat in sugar.

3. Add the vanilla and blend until smooth.

4. Separate the icing into two batches. Dye one batch green and frost the carrot greens part of the cake. Dye the other batch orange and frost the carrot part of the cake. Feel free to use a pastry bag for the greens part to make a leafy texture. Or use a toothpick to draw in the texture.

SPIDERWEBSOUP

The next time you meet a spider, ask him to weave you some Spider Web Soup. No two bowls are exactly alike.

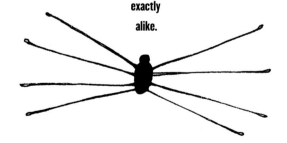

2 tablespoons butter

1/2 onion, finely chopped

1/2 cup celery, finely chopped

2 tablespoons flour

2-1/2 cups canned pureed tomatoes

2 cups vegetable or chicken stock

salt and pepper

1/4 cup sour cream

1 teaspoon milk

METHOD

1. In a soup pot over medium heat, melt the butter. Add the onions and celery, and cook about 8–10 minutes, until onions are clear.

2. Add the flour and stir about 5 minutes.

3. Add the tomatoes and the stock, and stir. Cook until smooth and boiling (about 10 minutes). Add salt and pepper to taste.

4. When you are ready to serve the soup, pour it into a serving bowl.

5. Mix the sour cream and milk together and pour into a squeeze bottle.

6. Using the squeeze bottle, squeeze out the sour cream and milk mixture into a small circle at the center of the bowl of soup. Make a larger circle around the first one, and continue making circles to the edge of the bowl.

7. Place a knife in the center of the soup and draw out to edge of bowl. Continue doing so around the soup to create spider web.

This is a nice soup to serve on a chilly, rainy, spooky evening.

Serves 2–4

MERINGUE MUSHROOMS

INGREDIENTS

2   egg whites

1/4 teaspoon vanilla extract

     pinch of salt

1/8 teaspoon cream of tartar

1/3 cup superfine sugar

1/4 cup chocolate chips

*Meringue Mushrooms are a sweet
accompaniment to a slice of
dirt-colored chocolate cake.*

Makes about 15 mushrooms

METHOD

1. Preheat the oven to 200°. Line two baking sheets with aluminum foil.

2. In a mixing bowl, beat the egg whites until foamy.

3. Add the vanilla, salt, and cream of tartar, and beat until soft peaks form.

4. Gradually add the sugar, 1 tablespoon at a time, beating for 30 seconds between each spoonful.

5. Continue beating until the egg whites are very stiff and glossy, but not dry.

6. Spoon the mixture into two pastry bags. Fit the bags with one large tip (5/8"–1") and one slightly smaller tip (1/2"). Make different-sized mushrooms, using a variety of tips if you wish.

7. Holding the larger-tipped bag near the baking sheet, squeeze out mounds to resemble mushroom caps. With a clean finger, smooth out any points on top of the caps.

8. Holding the smaller-tipped bag near the baking sheet, squeeze out a short stem (about 1"). Twist the bag to cut the mixture.

9. Baking time can vary, due to different ovens and different weather conditions. Usually it takes 2 to 2-1/2 hours for the mushrooms to bake. Make sure they are dry to the touch, crisp, and can be removed from the foil. To test a mushroom, remove a cap from the oven and cut it in half to make sure it is not gooey inside.

10. Remove the mushrooms from the oven and let them cool. Carefully trim any points off the stems with a knife.

11. In a double boiler (or the microwave), melt the chocolate chips. Dip the tip of the stem into the chocolate and attach to the top of the mushroom.

12. Let mushrooms dry upside down for about an hour. An empty egg carton is a good tray for drying mushrooms.

CAKE INGREDIENTS

1 recipe Master Chocolate Cake (page 106)

small terra-cotta pots

METHOD

1. Line terra-cotta pots with aluminum foil.

2. Follow the directions for the Master Chocolate Cake recipe.

3. Fill the terra-cotta pots three-quarters full with the cake batter. Bake 15–20 minutes or until a toothpick inserted into the center of the cake comes out clean. Let cakes cool completely.

ICING INGREDIENTS

1   cup butter, softened

3/4 cup cocoa

4   cups powdered sugar

1   teaspoon vanilla extract

2   tablespoons milk

3   cups chocolate cookies, crushed

5   flowers (Gerbera daisies, zinnias, or other flowers with long, sturdy stems work best.)

METHOD

1. In a medium mixing bowl, cream together the butter, cocoa, and powdered sugar.

2. Add the vanilla extract and milk, and blend until smooth.

3. Frost the cakes. Sprinkle the crushed chocolate cookies on top to resemble dirt.

4. Wrap the bottom of the flowers in aluminum foil and insert into the flower pots.

This is a delightful dessert to serve at a shower, tea, or other gracious occasion.

Makes 5 flower pots

FLOWERPOTCAKES

MOM ALWAYS TOLD YOU NOT TO PLAY IN THE DIRT. SHE PROBABLY WON'T MIND IF YOU DIG INTO FLOWER POT CAKES, THOUGH.

ANAT

HANDWICHES   MONSTER HEAD POTATOES   SPAGHETTI WITH EYEBA

ATOMICAL HEART COOKIES MARZIPAN FEET GINGERBREAD SKELETONS HAND PUNCH EYEBALL SNACKS FINGER COOKIES

HANDWICHES
ARE AN
UNEXPECTED
AND HELPFUL
PAIR OF HANDS
AT THE TABLE.
LET THEM GUIDE
YOU TO A
NICE LUNCH.

HANDWICHES

INGREDIENTS

4   slices of bread

assortment of your favorite sandwich meats

assortment of your favorite cheeses, thinly sliced

mayonnaise and mustard

hand-shaped cookie cutter (optional)

METHOD

1. Using the cookie cutter or a small knife, cut the bread into hand shapes.

2. Stack a few slices of meat and cheese on a cutting board. Cut these slices into the same shape as the bread.

3. Spread your favorite condiment(s) on the slices of bread. Place the meat and cheese hands between the bread hands.

Makes 2 hands

MONSTERHEAD POTATOES

POTATOES

BEFORE YOU GO TO SLEEP, BE SURE TO CHECK UNDER THE BED FOR ANY MONSTER HEAD POTATOES.

INGREDIENTS

1	head broccoli cut into florets
1	mushroom
2	asparagus spears
1/2	red pepper, cut into lip-shaped slices
1	tablespoon vegetable oil
2	radishes
2	black olive slices
2	peas
6	baking potatoes, peeled
2	teaspoons salt
1/3	cup milk or heavy cream
3	tablespoons butter
1	teaspoon pepper
1/4	cup canned corn

METHOD

1. Steam broccoli until cooked (5–10 minutes). Sauté the mushroom, asparagus, and red pepper slices in the oil if you don't like them raw.

2. To make the eyeballs, peel the radishes, leaving thin strips of skin in place for the eye veins. Slice off one end of the radishes to make a flat surface. Place a black olive slice with a pea in the center on the flat end of the radish.

3. Bring a large pot of water to a boil.

4. Peel off potato skins with a vegetable peeler. Cut the potatoes into quarters and put them in the large pot of boiling water. Add 1 teaspoon salt to the water, cover the pot, and boil 15–20 minutes, or until the potatoes are soft.

5. Remove from heat. Using a slotted spoon, scoop the potatoes out of the water and place them in a large mixing bowl. Add the milk, butter, pepper, and the remaining teaspoon of salt.

6. Mash the potatoes with a potato masher and stir until fluffy. Allow potatoes to cool slightly. With very clean hands, sculpt a head on a big serving platter.

7. Place broccoli on top of head for hair.

8. Make a mouth with the red peppers, and add the corn for teeth.

9. Attach the mushroom to make the nose.

10. Affix eyeballs, and place asparagus above them for eyebrows.

Serves 4–6

INGREDIENTS

vegetable oil

pinch each of salt and pepper

1 pound ground beef

1 jar (6 ounces) of pimento-stuffed olives

1/2 cup bread crumbs

1 pound spaghetti

1 egg, lightly beaten

1 jar (26 ounces) of spaghetti sauce

1 clove garlic, minced

Parmesan cheese (grated)

METHOD

1. Preheat the oven to 400°. Coat a baking sheet with the oil.

2. With your hands, mix the beef, bread crumbs, egg, garlic, salt, and pepper in a large bowl until well blended.

3. Shape into 1-1/2" balls, and insert one olive (pimento side "looking" out) into each ball. Place on the baking sheet three inches apart and bake about 15–20 minutes.

4. Bring a large pot of salted water to boil. Add the spaghetti to the water and cook according to the directions on the box. Drain the spaghetti in a colander over the sink.

5. Meanwhile, heat the spaghetti sauce in a pot over medium heat. Stir in the meatballs and let simmer for a few minutes. Serve the sauce over the spaghetti, and place two meatballs, eyes up, on each plate. Sprinkle Parmesan cheese over spaghetti.

Remember to serve eyeballs in pairs to your guests.

Serves 4–6

SPAGHETTI WITH EYEBALLS

THE PARTY'S OVER, AND LOOK AT WHAT'S LEFT ON THE BANQUET TABLE—
SPAGHETTI WITH EYEBALLS, OF COURSE. INTIMIDATING THE GUESTS WITH
HIS WILD-EYED STARE, HE'S THE LAST PARTY GUEST TO LEAVE.

ANATOMICAL HEARTCOOKIES

IF SOMEONE REALLY LOVES YOU, THEY WILL LOVE YOUR INSIDES, TOO. GIVE YOUR LOVED ONE THE TEST BY OFFERING THEM A COOKIE REPLICA OF WHAT YOUR HEART REALLY LOOKS LIKE.

COOKIE INGREDIENTS

3/4	cup butter, softened	1	teaspoon baking powder
1-3/4	cups sugar	1/4	teaspoon salt
2	eggs	2–3	tablespoons ice water
4	cups flour		

METHOD

1. Preheat the oven to 400°. In a large mixing bowl, cream the butter. Add the sugar gradually, creaming well.

2. Add the eggs and water and blend.

3. Sift the flour with baking powder and salt and add to the creamed mixture. Blend thoroughly.

4. Roll the dough into a thin layer on a lightly floured surface.

5. With a small sharp knife, cut into heart shapes (refer to photograph).

6. With a spatula, carefully transfer the hearts to an ungreased baking sheet. Bake 7–8 minutes, until the edges are just beginning to brown.

Give an Anatomical Heart Cookie to someone you love for Valentine's Day.

Makes about 30–40 hearts

ICING INGREDIENTS

2 cups powdered sugar

1 teaspoon vanilla extract

3 tablespoons water
  red food coloring

1 tube red decorating icing

1 tube blue decorating icing

METHOD

1. In a medium mixing bowl, mix together the powdered sugar, vanilla, water, and 1–2 drops red food coloring.

2. Ice the cookies.

3. When the pink icing has set, draw in veins with the tubes of red and blue decorating icing.

MARZIPANFEET

IT IS SO EXCITING TO WITNESS SOMEONE'S VERY FIRST STEPS, ESPECIALLY WHEN THEY ARE MADE BY DELECTABLE MARZIPAN FEET!

INGREDIENTS

1 roll (7 ounces) prepared marzipan
  red food coloring

METHOD

1. Pinch off a 2-inch piece of marzipan from the roll. Make marzipan malleable by rolling it between hands and kneading it slightly.

2. Using your hands, mold the marzipan into the shape of a foot. Use toothpicks and a butter knife to define the toes and toenails.

3. Using a toothpick dipped in the red food coloring, give your marzipan feet a pedicure.

Makes 4 feet

GINGERBREAD
SKELETONS

GINGERBREAD SKELETONS CAN BE FOUND IN DESSERTS AROUND THE WORLD.

INGREDIENTS

1/2	cup sugar
1/2	cup butter
1/2	cup molasses
1/4	cup water
2-1/2	cups flour, sifted
3/4	teaspoon salt
1/4	teaspoon nutmeg
1/2	teaspoon baking soda
3/4	teaspoon ginger
1/8	teaspoon allspice
	animal and gingerbread people cookie cutters
1	tube white decorating icing with small tip

METHOD

1. In a large mixing bowl, cream the sugar and butter together. Add molasses and water.

2. In a separate bowl, mix the flour, salt, nutmeg, baking soda, ginger, and allspice. Gradually add the dry mixture to the wet and blend until the dough holds together.

3. Cover and chill for 2–3 hours.

4. Preheat the oven to 375°.

5. Roll out dough 1/4" thick on a lightly floured surface.

6. Cut into shapes with cookie cutters and transfer to cookie sheet.

7. Bake for 10–12 minutes. Remove from the oven and let cool on baking sheets or cooling racks.

8. Using the white decorating icing, decorate the cookies with "bones" so that they resemble skeletons.

You could serve these on a plate of light brown sugar to resemble a desert.

Makes about 15–20 cookies, depending on the size of the cookie cutters

FLOATING RED

HANDS IN YOUR

FRUITY PUNCH

WILL SURELY

GET A ROUND

OF APPLAUSE.

HANDPUNCH

INGREDIENTS

4 latex surgical gloves,
   unpowdered

1 can (12 ounces) cranberry juice

1 can (12 ounces) lemonade

2 cans (24 ounces) pineapple juice

METHOD

1. Fill the surgical gloves with cranberry juice. Tie a knot at the end, or secure the gloves with a rubber band. Place them in the freezer overnight.

2. In a large punch bowl, mix the lemonade and pineapple juice together.

3. Carefully peel the surgical gloves off the frozen cranberry hands. Place the hands in the punch.

These icy hands will help keep your punch cool as well as spook your guests. Recommended for Halloween.

Serves 15–20

EYEBALLSNACKS

HAVE YOU EVER FELT LIKE YOU WERE BEING WATCHED? EYEBALL SNACKS WERE PROBABLY IN THE ROOM.

INGREDIENTS

1   dozen eggs
    pitted black olives
    salt and pepper

METHOD

1. In a pot, cover eggs in cold water. Place on stove and bring water to a boil.

2. Reduce the heat to low and cook for 12 minutes.

3. Remove from the heat and run the eggs under cold water.

4. Peel the eggs and slice in half.

5. Slice the olives into quarters and place one quarter on each egg "iris." Sprinkle salt and pepper on each egg to taste.

Serve in pairs and watch your back!

Makes 12 pairs of eyes

COOKIE INGREDIENTS

1 cup butter, softened

1 cup powdered sugar

1 egg

1 teaspoon vanilla extract

2-3/4 cups all-purpose flour

1 teaspoon baking powder

1 teaspoon salt

1/2 cup sliced almonds

2 tablespoons Icing Glue (see below)

ICING GLUE INGREDIENTS

1/4 cup powdered sugar

1 teaspoon water

METHOD

Mix together in a small bowl until the consistency is similar to that of a paste.

METHOD

1. In a large mixing bowl, beat the butter until smooth and creamy.

2. Add the sugar, egg, and vanilla extract and mix well.

3. Add the flour, baking powder, and salt and beat until completely mixed.

4. Cover the dough and refrigerate for 30 minutes.

5. Preheat the oven to 325°.

6. With your hands, roll a heaping tablespoon of dough into a finger shape for each cookie. If the dough gets sticky and hard to work with, put it back in the refrigerator for a little while. Place fingers on an ungreased cookie sheet about 3 inches apart.

7. Use a butter knife to make knuckle marks on the finger cookies. Slightly flatten the front of the finger to create a nail.

8. Bake 20–25 minutes, until fingers are slightly golden. Remove from the oven and let cool. Meanwhile, prepare the Icing Glue.

9. Attach almond slice fingernails to the tips of the fingers with Icing Glue. Let glue dry for about 30 minutes.

This is a good cookie to make for Halloween.

Makes about 50 fingers

FINGER COOKIES ARE USUALLY FOUND IN SETS OF FIVE. IF YOU THINK THEY LOOK WEIRD, YOU SHOULD SEE THE COOKIE PERSON TO WHOM THESE FINGERS ONCE BELONGED.

FINGER COOKIES

JELL-O AQUARIUM   FRUIT PIZZA   SU

PCAKES   SOLAR SYSTEM MINTS   PANTS AND SHIRT CAKES   LICORICE RECORDS   FOOTBALL MEATLOAF   BURRITO PRESENTS

IT IS SUCH A PEACEFUL FEELING TO GAZE INTO A BEAUTIFUL BLUE FISHBOWL. WHY ARE THESE LOVELY FISH SO STILL, THOUGH? FOR DINNER PARTIES, THIS AQUARIUM MAKES A MESMERIZING CENTERPIECE.

JELL-OAQUARIUM

INGREDIENTS

1-1/2 gallon glass goldfish bowl

2 boxes (6 ounces) Berry Blue Jell-O gelatin

1 can (11 ounces) fruit cocktail

2 gummy fish (or plastic fish)

1 plastic aquarium plant (optional)

METHOD

1. Make the Jell-O gelatin according to directions on the box. Pour into goldfish bowl.

2. Drain the fruit cocktail and slowly pour it into the goldfish bowl. It will sink to the bottom to act as the "gravel."

3. Place Jell-O gelatin in the refrigerator to thicken, for about an hour. Don't let it set completely.

4. Remove from the refrigerator and place the gummy (or plastic) fish in the Jell-O gelatin, using a chopstick, knife, or the back of a spoon to push the fish toward the bottom of the goldfish bowl.

5. Return the Jell-O gelatin to the refrigerator to set completely.

6. When the Jell-O gelatin has set and is ready to serve, use a spoon to scoop it and the fish out. If you are using plastic fish, be sure to set them aside.

This recipe can also be made in small individual goldfish bowls, so that guests can take them home as party favors. If you want to make the "water" in your aquarium a lighter shade of blue, you can replace the second box of Berry Blue Jell-O gelatin with four 7-gram packets of unflavored gelatin.

Serves 6–8

FRUITPIZZA

IT'S GAME TIME! INVITE THE BUDDIES OVER, GET SETTLED ON THE SOFA, FLIP ON THE TV, AND ENJOY A FRUIT PIZZA.

INGREDIENTS

1   cup butter, softened

1/2 cup powdered sugar

2   cups flour

1   package (8 ounces) cream cheese

1   can (14 ounces) condensed milk

1/4 cup lemon juice

     raspberry (without seeds) or strawberry jam in a squeeze bottle

     fresh fruit of your choice

METHOD

1. Preheat the oven to 325°.

2. Cream the butter in a large mixing bowl. Gradually add the sugar and flour, and mix well.

3. Using your fingertips or the heel of your hand, press out the dough into a pizza pan, or roll it flat into a circle on a cookie sheet.

4. Bake the dough 15–20 minutes, until the crust is golden brown. Remove from the oven and let cool.

5. Mix the cream cheese together with the condensed milk and lemon juice. Spread over the crust.

6. Squeeze the jam onto the edge of the cream cheese to resemble tomato sauce.

7. Cut up the fruit and arrange on the pizza. Chill until ready to serve.

Serve in slices like pizza.

Serves 6–8

CUPCAKE INGREDIENTS

1 recipe Master Yellow Cake (page 107)

METHOD

1. Grease and flour cupcake tins.

2. Follow the recipe for the Master Yellow Cake.

3. Fill the cupcake tins three-quarters full with batter.

4. Bake until a toothpick inserted into the center comes out clean, approximately 12–15 minutes. Let the cupcakes cool completely.

Make your own favorite type of sushi cupcakes by using different candies. For a party, create a whole sushi platter.

Makes 12–15 cupcakes

ICING INGREDIENTS

1-1/2	cups sour cream
3/4	teaspoon vanilla
4-1/2	cups shredded coconut
3/4	cup powdered sugar, sifted

METHOD

1. In a medium mixing bowl, combine the sour cream, vanilla, and coconut.

2. Add the powdered sugar to the mixture and mix thoroughly.

3. Using a butter knife, spread the icing over the tops of the cupcakes.

DECORATION INGREDIENTS

8   green Fruit Roll-Ups fruit snacks

assorted candies (jelly beans, gummy worms, gummy fish)

dried papaya and mangoes

METHOD

1. Trim the Fruit Roll-Ups to the height of the cupcakes. Wrap one fruit roll around the side of each cupcake.

2. Arrange the dried papaya and candies on the tops of the cupcakes.

3. Serve the dried mangoes on the side to resemble ginger.

SUSHICUPCAKES

GIVEN AS A GIFT IN A BENTO BOX, SUSHI CUPCAKES ARE CONSIDERED A SIGN OF SPECIAL CONSIDERATION OR RESPECT. THESE EXOTIC SWEETS MAY BE EATEN WITH CHOPSTICKS OR WITHOUT.

SOLARSYSTEMMINTS

IN THE DARK OF NIGHT, THE JEWEL-LIKE PLANETS OF OUR SOLAR SYSTEM APPEAR IN THE SKY. WHO EVER IMAGINED THAT YOU COULD EAT THEM AS A TREAT?

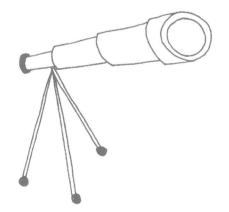

INGREDIENTS

1-1/2 tablespoons butter, softened

1-1/2 tablespoons light corn syrup

1/4   teaspoon salt

3/4   teaspoon mint extract

2   cups powdered sugar

food coloring (various colors)

METHOD

1. In a medium bowl, use a fork to mix together the butter, corn syrup, salt, and mint extract.

2. Gradually add the powdered sugar, and continue stirring. When the dough becomes too stiff to stir, knead it with your hands.

3. Create the planets by rolling different-sized balls of the dough between your hands. Using food coloring and a small clean paintbrush, paint the planets.

4. Store in the refrigerator to keep fresh, up to two weeks.

Serve our solar system on a plate to your friends in the evening while stargazing.

Makes 1 complete solar system (9 planets)

PANTSANDSHIRTCAKES

WHAT A CUTE OUTFIT THE PANTS AND SHIRT CAKES MAKE.
PLEASE AVOID DRY CLEANING.

PANTS CAKE INGREDIENTS

1 recipe Master Chocolate Cake
(page 106)

METHOD

1. Grease and flour a 9" x 13" pan.
   Follow the recipe for the Master
   Chocolate Cake.

2. Bake about 30 minutes, or until a
   toothpick inserted into the center
   of the cake comes out clean.
   Remove from the oven, let sit for
   a few minutes, then turn the cake
   onto a rack to cool completely.

3. Place the cake on a large board
   to frost. Cut a triangle out of the
   bottom half to make the pants legs.

SHIRT CAKE INGREDIENTS

1 recipe Master Yellow Cake
(page 107)

METHOD

1. Grease and flour a 9" x 13" pan.
   Follow the recipe for the Master
   Yellow Cake.

2. Bake about 30 minutes, or until a
   toothpick inserted into the center
   of cake comes out clean. Remove
   from the oven, let sit for a few
   minutes, then turn the cake onto
   a rack to cool completely.

3. Slice the bottom quarter of the
   cake off to make a square. Cut the
   sliced-off rectangle in half and
   attach both pieces to the sides of
   the remaining square to resemble
   sleeves. Cut a small sliver out of
   the top for the neckline.

ICING INGREDIENTS

2 batches of Master Butter-Cream Icing
recipe (page 107)

Food coloring (various colors)

METHOD

1. Using food coloring, mix colors
   for the pants and shirt. Remember
   it's okay to mix and match stripes,
   plaids, and polka dots.

2. Frost the cakes.

*Guests will love that they can choose
chocolate or yellow cake (or both).
For an added stylish accent, present
them in empty, foil-lined shirt boxes.*

Serves about 20

LICORICERECORDS

WHATEVER YOUR MUSICAL TASTE, THESE TINY DISKS REALLY ROCK OUT. PUT ON YOUR DANCING SHOES WHEN SERVING.

INGREDIENTS

6 small disk-shaped candies

6 Fruit Roll-Ups fruit snacks

6 black licorice whips

1 tablespoon honey

METHOD

1. With a toothpick, carefully poke a hole into the center of each disk-shaped candy.

2. Unroll the Fruit Roll-Ups and dampen them slightly with a little bit of water and a paper towel.

3. Wind the licorice into a round shape on the Fruit Roll-Up. The fruit roll will stick to the licorice, creating a base for the candy.

4. Trim the edge of the fruit roll around the licorice.

5. Affix the candy to the licorice record with a little honey.

Snack on these while listening to your favorite tunes.

Makes 6 records

AH, THE CHILL IN THE AIR, THE GLARE OF THE STADIUM LIGHTS, THE GREEN OF THE ASTROTURF, AND THE TASTE OF MEATLOAF. IT'S FOOTBALL SEASON.

FOOTBALLMEATLOAF

INGREDIENTS

	vegetable oil	1	egg, slightly beaten
1-1/2	pounds ground turkey	1	teaspoon Worcestershire sauce
1/4	cup bread crumbs	1/2	teaspoon pepper
1	envelope dry onion soup	1	white onion, cut in half and sliced
1	can (6 ounces) evaporated milk		

METHOD

1. Preheat the oven to 350°. Grease a shallow pan with vegetable oil.

2. In a large bowl, mix all the ingredients together, except for the onion slices. Use your hands to mix the ingredients thoroughly.

3. Using your hands, form the mixture into a football shape and place it in the oiled pan.

4. Bake for 1 hour.

5. Place the onion slices on the football in a stitching pattern.

Best served on Super Bowl Sunday, or to celebrate any important football game.

Serves 4–6

1 bunch green onions

1 leek, sliced lengthwise

2 tablespoons vegetable oil

1 cup tomato, chopped

1/4 cup onion, chopped

2 ounces green chili peppers, diced

1 teaspoon garlic powder

1/4 teaspoon salt

1 can (15 ounces) kidney beans, drained and mashed

1/2 cup grated cheddar cheese

6 flour tortillas (use different-colored tortillas—spinach and tomato—if you wish)

1. Preheat the oven to 350°.

2. Bring a medium pot of water to a boil, and dip the green onions and leeks in quickly with tongs. Let them cool on a plate.

3. In a large skillet, heat the vegetable oil over medium heat.

4. Add tomato, onion, green chilies, garlic powder, and salt to the skillet, and cook until the onions begin to brown, about 5 minutes.

5. Add the mashed beans and cheese, and mix well.

6. Wrap the tortillas in aluminum foil and heat in the oven for 10 minutes.

7. Remove the tortillas from the oven. Spoon a scoop of the bean mixture into the center of the tortilla and wrap. Fold the horizontal sides in toward each other, and roll the burrito up toward you.

8. Place the burrito on a plate or serving dish. Wrap one leek around the width of the burrito, then another around the length. Tuck the ends of the leek underneath the burrito. Tie a simple bow with the green onion or another leek at the spot where the leeks cross on the burrito.

Burritos are an ideal birthday meal.

Serves 6

BURRITOPRESENTS

GIVE THE THOUGHTFUL GIFT OF BEANS: SWEETLY WRAPPED BURRITOS TIED WITH PRETTY, EDIBLE RIBBON.

ANG
KING

BIRDS' NESTS CHOCOLATE MICE POND

IMAL
DOM

JELL-O EGGS   MUTANT CHICKEN   MONKEY POPS   DINOSAUR DIP   BIRD BIRTHDAY CAKE   SHEEP IN BLANKETS   CHOCOLATE MOOSE

INGREDIENTS

spray-on cooking oil

3   cups miniature marshmallows

3   tablespoons butter (plus 1
    teaspoon for your hands)

4   cups chow mein noodles

12 yogurt-covered almonds
    or jelly beans

METHOD

1. Line a cookie sheet with aluminum foil. Coat well with spray-on cooking oil.

2. In a saucepan, melt the marshmallows and butter together over medium heat. Stir until smooth.

3. Put the noodles in a large mixing bowl. Pour the marshmallow mixture over the noodles. Stir until well coated.

4. Rub butter on your hands and form about four balls out of the noodle mixture. Place on cookie sheet.

5. With the back of a spoon, press the center of each ball to make an indentation.

6. Let the nests set until firm. Fill with yogurt-covered almonds or jelly beans for the birds' eggs.

Makes 4–6 nests

BIRDS'NESTS
BIRDS WILL SOMETIMES BUILD THEIR NESTS OUT OF THE STRANGEST THINGS.

CHOCOLATE MICE

BE VERY QUIET AND YOU MAY HEAR THE SCURRYING OF TINY CHOCOLATE MICE
AS THEY BUILD THEIR NEST. LET'S HOPE A CHOCOLATE CAT DOESN'T FIND THEM.

INGREDIENTS

4   (1 ounce) squares
    semisweet chocolate

1/3 cup sour cream

1   cup finely crushed chocolate
    wafer cookies

1/3 cup cocoa powder

1/3 cup powdered sugar

1/4 cup sliced almonds

    small candies of your choice
    for eyes and noses

    black whip licorice for tails

METHOD

1. In a double boiler (or the microwave), melt the chocolate, stirring thoroughly.
   Cover and refrigerate until cool and firm, about 20 minutes.

2. In a large mixing bowl, combine the chocolate with the sour cream.

3. Add the chocolate wafer crumbs and mix well.

4. Roll teaspoons of dough into a slight oval shape. Mold one end to a
   slight point for the nose.

5. Put cocoa and powdered sugar in separate small bowls. Roll each oval
   in cocoa powder for dark mice or in powdered sugar for white mice.

6. On each mouse, press in candies for the eyes and nose, and almond slices
   for the ears. Attach a licorice whip for a tail.

7. Refrigerate for at least 2 hours until firm.

*Try making a whole mouse family with babies. These would be fun
to have at an event where you also serve cheese.*

Makes about 10 mice

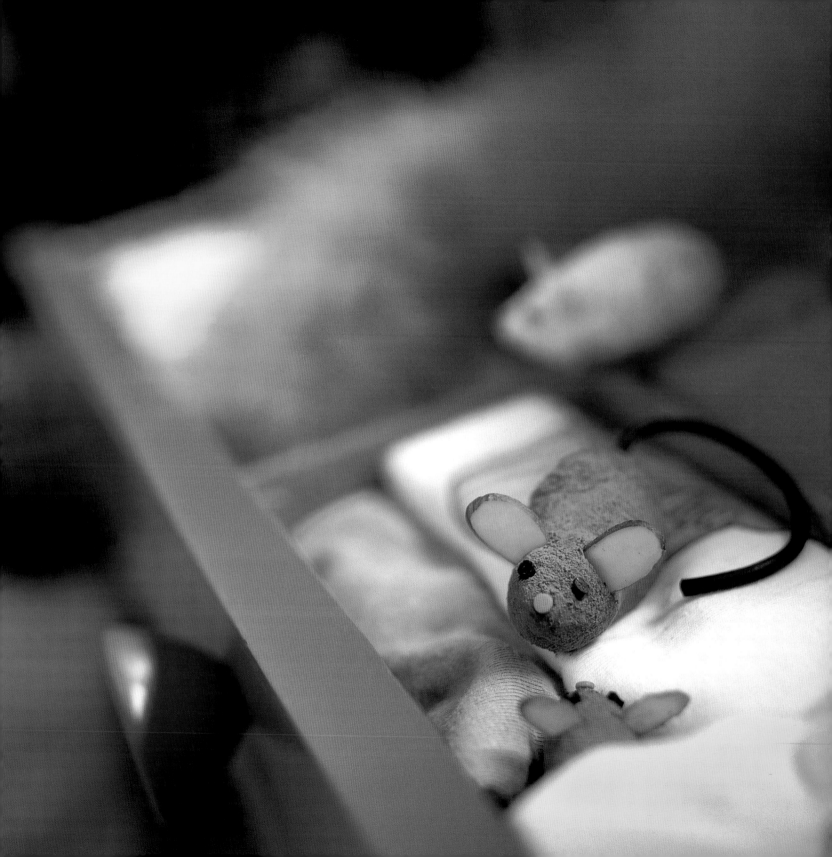

INGREDIENTS

4   tablespoons butter, melted

1   cup chocolate cookie crumbs

1   box (6 ounces) vanilla-flavored pudding

    milk, if called for on the
    pudding box

1   cup heavy cream, whipped

1   teaspoon peppermint extract

    green food coloring

    assorted herbs (fennel, rosemary, sage, thyme)

    a small plastic frog, snake, turtle, or duck

METHOD

1. Mix the butter and cookie crumbs together in a bowl. Press the mixture into a 9" pie pan. Chill in the refrigerator while you prepare the filling.

2. Make the pudding according to the pie-filling recipe on the box.

3. Blend the whipped cream and peppermint extract into the pudding.

4. Add a few drops of green food coloring to the pudding to make your "water" pond colored. Spoon into the pie tin. Chill in the refrigerator about 1 hour.

5. Add the herbs along the muddy banks of your pond, and place the small swamp animal in the center.

Serves 6–8

ARE WE IN A SWAMP?

NO, WE ARE IN A SWEET,

DELICIOUS POND PIE.

THANKFULLY,

THE ALLIGATORS

HERE DON'T BITE.

PONDPIE

IMAGINE WHAT SORT OF CRAZY BIRD WOULD LEAVE THESE PRECIOUS EGGS BEHIND FOR SOME HUNGRY HIKER TO FIND. THEIR BRIGHT COLORS DON'T CAMOUFLAGE THEM VERY WELL, DO THEY?

JELL-O EGGS

INGREDIENTS

8 eggs

1 package (3 ounces) Jell-O gelatin, any flavor

METHOD

1. With a skewer or a metal cake tester, make a 1/2-inch hole in the top of each egg. Shake the whites and yolks out of the shells.

2. Rinse the shells thoroughly with warm soapy water. Then rinse thoroughly with warm water only. Place the eggshells back in the egg carton.

3. Make the Jell-O gelatin according to the instructions on the box. Using a tiny funnel or a measuring cup with a spout, carefully pour the gelatin into the eggshells.

4. Chill until firm.

5. Once they're chilled, crack the shells slightly. Dip the eggs very quickly in a bowl of warm water, and peel off the shells.

No springtime party is complete without them.

Makes 8 eggs

INGREDIENTS

1 whole roasting chicken

2 extra drumsticks

olive oil

salt

pepper

garlic powder

sturdy toothpicks, short skewers, or poultry needle and thread

METHOD

1. Preheat the oven to 450°.

2. Rub the chicken and extra drumsticks with olive oil. Sprinkle salt, pepper, and garlic powder on the skin. Place the chicken and the drumsticks on a rack in an uncovered pan, and put them in the oven. Reduce the heat to 350°.

3. Roast about 20 minutes per pound of chicken. The drumsticks will be done more quickly, in 1 hour. Remove the drumsticks from the oven when ready.

4. Allow the chicken to cool 10 minutes. Then attach the legs to the body of the chicken with toothpicks, skewers, or a poultry needle, and thread before serving.

To test the chicken for doneness, prick it where the drumsticks attach to the body with a toothpick or sharp knife. When the juices run clear, the chicken is ready. You can do the same test with the extra drumsticks.

Serves 4–6

MUTANTCHICKEN

THE MUTANT CHICKEN WAS THE FASTEST ONE IN THE BARNYARD. NOW THAT IT'S ON THE DINNER TABLE, THERE ARE TWO MORE DELICIOUS DRUMSTICKS TO ENJOY FOR SUNDAY DINNER.

MONKEYPOPS

THE DEEP FOREST IS WHERE THE MONKEY POPS LIVE. YOU CAN HEAR THEM SWINGING FROM TREE TO TREE AND LAUGHING THEIR CHOCOLATE HEADS OFF.

INGREDIENTS

8	wooden craft sticks
4	firm, ripe bananas, cut in half
16	sliced almonds
2	cups semisweet chocolate chips
1-1/2	tablespoons vegetable oil
16	small round candies (for eyes)
8	maraschino cherries, sliced into smile shapes
16	sesame seeds

METHOD

1. Line a cookie sheet with waxed paper.

2. Insert one craft stick into the flat (sliced) end of each banana half. To make the ears, insert an almond slice into each side of the pointy end of the banana half.

3. In a double boiler (or the microwave), melt the chocolate chips. Stir in the vegetable oil.

4. Remove the chocolate from the heat. Place bananas on a rack with waxed paper or a tray underneath. Spoon the chocolate over bananas. Place the bananas on the cookie sheet.

5. Press the candy eyes, cherry mouths, and sesame seed nostrils onto the faces of the monkeys.

6. Freeze at least an hour before serving.

Have a monkey puppet show before eating.

Makes 8 monkeys

DINOSAURDIP

DELICIOUS DINOSAUR DIP WILL NEVER BECOME EXTINCT. YOUR GUESTS WILL ASK FOR IT AGAIN AND AGAIN.

DINOSAUR INGREDIENTS

1   acorn squash

1   zucchini

4   small pickling cucumbers

1   small green pepper or okra

   toothpicks

   cloves or peppercorns

METHOD

1. Cut the acorn squash in half. Scoop out the seeds.

2. Slice the top two inches off the zucchini at an angle. Attach this section back onto the zucchini with toothpicks to make the head of the dinosaur. Slice the other end of the zucchini at an angle and attach it with toothpicks to the acorn squash half.

3. Cut a small notch in the zucchini for the mouth and insert cloves for the eyes. Pin the four pickling cucumbers to the squash with toothpicks for legs.

4. Using a toothpick, attach the pepper or okra to the rear of the dinosaur for a tail.

DIP INGREDIENTS

1   cup sour cream

2   tablespoons fresh dill, chopped

1   teaspoon onion powder

   salt and pepper to taste

METHOD

1. Mix all the ingredients together in a small bowl. Chill until you're ready to serve.

2. Spoon into the dinosaur's belly.

PALM TREE INGREDIENTS

Carrots, unpeeled and washed

Green bell peppers

METHOD

1. Cut off the bottoms of the carrots evenly so they will stand up.

2. With a small knife, make one-inch incisions one-eighth of an inch thick randomly around the carrot to create scales. Place the carrots in a bowl of ice water. The scales will separate from the carrots so they will resemble tree trunks.

3. Cut the tops off of the green peppers in a zigzag pattern. Cut a small hole out of the tip of the pepper and attach to the end of the standing carrot with a toothpick.

Place prehistoric trees around your dinosaur for dipping.

Serves 6–8

INGREDIENTS

vegetable oil or shortening

1   cup birdseed

1/2 cup honey

peanut butter

sunflower seeds (unsalted)

METHOD

1. Wash out an empty 6-ounce can (a tuna can works well) and an empty 3-ounce can. Grease the cans with oil or shortening.

2. In a small saucepan, combine the birdseed and honey and cook over medium heat while stirring. When the honey starts to boil, cook about 5 minutes, stirring constantly. The honey should darken slightly.

3. Remove from heat, and spoon the birdseed mixture into the cans. Refrigerate until the mixture hardens, about two hours.

4. With a can opener, remove the bottoms from the cans. Gently press the cakes out onto a plate.

5. Stack the smaller cake piece on top of the larger cake piece. Decorate the cake with peanut butter and sunflower seeds.

This little cake is strictly for the birds, not people.

Makes one cake

BIRDBIRTHDAYCAKE

BIRDS HAVE BIRTHDAYS, TOO. CELEBRATE THIS SPECIAL OCCASION BY GIVING THEM A TASTY LITTLE CAKE IN THEIR FAVORITE TREE.

INGREDIENTS

1   can crescent roll dough

7   small cocktail sausages

14 peppercorns

METHOD

1. Preheat the oven to 375°.

2. Unroll the dough. Using one section of the dough, pinch off 14 tiny pieces and 7 slightly larger pieces. These will be used to make the sheep's ears and tails.

3. Wrap the remaining sections of dough around the sausages blanket-style, using one section of dough per sausage. If necessary, make the sections of dough smaller so that they don't overwhelm the sausage. Close the dough around one end of the sausage, leaving the other end sticking out.

4. Create two ears on each sheep by attaching the tiny balls of dough to the edge of the wrapped blanket. Create the tails by placing the larger pieces of dough on the closed end of the wrapped blanket.

5. Place the sheep on a cookie sheet two inches apart and bake 12–15 minutes, until the dough is golden brown.

6. With a toothpick, poke two holes in the sausages and insert two peppercorns to make the sheep's eyes.

These make a great after-school snack. If you want legs on your sheep, add a few extra sausages to the baking sheet. Once removed from the oven, cut off the ends of the sausages (about a centimeter on each side), and attach to the bottom of your sheep with half of a toothpick. Remember to tell your friends to remove the toothpicks before eating.

Makes 7 sheep

SHEEPINBLANKETS

ONE SHEEP, TWO SHEEP, THREE SHEEP... ARE COZY IN THEIR SOFT BLANKETS.
SOON THEY'LL BE ASLEEP AND DREAMING ABOUT SNACKS.

CHOCOLATEMOOSE

THE CHOCOLATE MOOSE IS A MAJESTIC AND REGAL BEAST
IN THE WOODS. WHO KNEW HE COULD BE SO SWEET?

INGREDIENTS

1	teaspoon unflavored gelatin
1	tablespoon cold water
2	tablespoons boiling water
1/2	cup white sugar
1/4	cup cocoa powder
1	cup heavy cream, chilled
1	teaspoon vanilla
8	white or tan pipe cleaners

METHOD

1. In a small bowl, sprinkle gelatin over cold water and let stand for one minute to soften. Add the boiling water and stir until gelatin is dissolved completely.

2. Stir together the sugar and cocoa in mixing bowl. Add the heavy cream and vanilla and beat until mixture is stiff.

3. Add the gelatin mixture and beat until well blended.

4. Spoon into parfait glasses and refrigerate for about 30 minutes before serving.

5. Meanwhile, bend the pipe cleaners into antler shapes. Make a pair for each parfait glass.

6. Remove parfait glasses from refrigerator and attach pairs of google eyes to them with a little bit of tack or tape. Stick two antlers in moose and serve.

Serves 4

IMER

TION

WAIIAN SHIRT PUNCH   PLAY-OFF CUPCAKES   CHERRY COLA   BAKED ICE-CREAM CONES   BANANA DOG   POSTCARD COOKIES

INGREDIENTS

4   smooth baking potatoes

1/2 cup olive oil

     salt and pepper to taste

32   medium-sized green beans

METHOD

1. Preheat the oven to 400°.

2. Wash and dry the potatoes. Cut the potatoes lengthwise into 1/4" slices.

3. Drizzle half of the olive oil onto a foil-lined cookie sheet. Place the potatoes on the cookie sheet and drizzle the remaining oil over them.

4. Sprinkle with salt and pepper and bake in the oven until the potatoes are tender and starting to brown (30–40 minutes).

5. Meanwhile, steam the green beans until bright green and still a little crunchy (about 5–10 minutes). Set aside.

6. Remove the potatoes from the oven. With a small knife or a chopstick, punch holes widthwise into the potato slices on either side of the potato, and one hole in the center at one end of the potato.

7. Insert the green beans into the holes to create straps for the flip-flops.

Serve in pairs as a side dish to a nice lunch or dinner, or as an appetizer at a party. If you like the taste of rosemary, sprinkle some on the potatoes before baking. It's also easy to add a little decoration to your flip-flops. Slice a carrot or radish into quarter-inch rounds. Cut tiny triangles out of the rounds to create flowers. Place a radish flower on top of the green bean straps where they form a V. Enjoy the fashion!

Makes 8 pairs of flip-flops

POTATO FLIP-FLOPS

FLIP, FLOP, FLIP, FLOP IS THE SOUND THAT POTATO FLIP-FLOPS MAKE AS THEY STEP ACROSS THE HOT CEMENT. THESE FASHIONABLE SUMMERTIME SHOES ARE ALWAYS EATEN IN MATCHING PAIRS.

HAWAIIAN SHIRTPUNCH

HOW HANDY TO HAVE A BRIGHT AND CHEERFUL HAWAIIAN SHIRT THAT YOU CAN ENJOY ON A HOT DAY. THIS IS A VERY BOLD FASHION STATEMENT TO MAKE AT A PARTY.

INGREDIENTS

1 can (12 ounces) pineapple juice

2 cans (14 ounces) cranberry juice

3 apples

3 kiwi fruits, peeled

1 cup blueberries

METHOD

1. Mix the juices together in a punch bowl.

2. Slice the apples and kiwi fruits crosswise.

3. With a small knife, cut five small triangle shapes out of each kiwi and apple slice to make the flowers for your "shirt."

4. Place the flowers (kiwi fruits and apples) and polka dots (blueberries) on your Hawaiian shirt (punch)!

Any kind of fruit that slices well will work in this punch. Use what's in season or your personal favorites, such as kumquats, strawberries, oranges, pears, or watermelon.

Serves 10–15

CUPCAKE INGREDIENTS

1 Master Yellow Cake recipe
(page 107)

METHOD

1. Place cupcake liners in muffin trays.

2. Follow the recipe for the Master Yellow Cake.

3. Fill the cupcake liners until three-quarters full and bake 10–12 minutes, or until the cake springs up when touched. Let the cupcakes cool before icing.

ICING INGREDIENTS

1 Master Butter-Cream Icing recipe
(page 107)

food coloring

1 tube each of black, red, yellow, and white decorating icing with small tip

METHOD

1. Follow the recipe for the Master Butter-Cream Icing.

2. Using food coloring, mix colors for the balls you like the most (white for baseballs, yellow for tennis balls, orange for basketballs).

3. Frost the cupcakes.

4. Using the decorating icing tubes, apply lines to decorate the balls.

Makes 12–14 cupcakes

PLAY-OFF CUPCAKES

SCORE ONE FOR THE TEAM WITH THESE SPORTY TREATS. THEY'RE A BIG HIT ON GAME DAY.

CHERRY**COLA**

CHERRY COLA IS A GOOD WAY TO HAVE YOUR COLD DRINK AND EAT IT, TOO.

INGREDIENTS

1   box (3 ounces) cherry gelatin
1   cup boiling water
1   cup cola drink
4   cherries
4   straws

METHOD

1. Dissolve gelatin in boiling water. Add cola and stir.

2. Pour into four small soda glasses.

3. Chill until set.

4. Garnish with cherries and straws.

Makes 4 glasses

BAKED ICE-CREAM CONES

THE MAGICAL THING ABOUT THESE ICE-CREAM CONES IS THAT THEY DON'T MELT IN THE BRIGHT SUMMER SUN. IN FACT, THESE ICE-CREAM CONES HAVE EVEN SPENT SOME TIME IN A HOT OVEN.

CAKE INGREDIENTS

12 wafer ice-cream cones with flat bottoms

1 recipe Master Chocolate Cake or Master Yellow Cake (pages 106–107)

METHOD

1. Preheat the oven to 350°.

2. Follow recipe for the Master Chocolate Cake or Yellow Cake.

3. Fill the ice-cream cones three-quarters full with batter.

4. Carefully set the cones on a baking sheet, or in a muffin tin, and place in the oven. Don't let the cones tip over.

5. Bake 15–20 minutes, until a toothpick inserted in the cake comes out clean.

ICING INGREDIENTS

1 recipe Master Butter-Cream Icing (page 107)

food coloring

sprinkles (optional)

METHOD

1. Follow the recipe for the Master Butter-Cream Icing.

2. Using food coloring, mix colors that look like ice cream (pink, brown, etc.).

3. Spoon the icing into a pastry bag that has a large tip. Swirl the frosting into the cone to make the icing look like soft-serve ice cream, or frost with a butter knife for that "scooped" ice cream look. Add sprinkles, if you wish.

Serve these un-melting ice-cream cones on a hot day.

Makes about 12 cones

THE BANANA DOG
LOVES PICNICS
AND BARBECUES.
BUT IF YOU'RE
LOOKING FOR
HIM AROUND A GRILL,
YOU'RE BARKING
UP THE WRONG TREE.

BANANADOG

INGREDIENTS

1   hot dog bun

1   tablespoon strawberry or raspberry jam

1   tablespoon peanut butter

1   banana

METHOD

1. Spread the jam on one side of the hot dog bun to resemble ketchup.

2. Spread the peanut butter on the other side of the hot dog bun to resemble mustard. (Put the peanut butter in a yellow squeeze bottle, if you like.)

3. Place banana in bun.

Serve this easy snack at a summertime BBQ and surprise your guests.

Serves 1

POSTCARDCOOKIES

EVERYONE LOVES GETTING A POSTCARD. THIS ONE IS PROBABLY FROM SOMEONE ON VACATION IN A FARAWAY KITCHEN.

COOKIE INGREDIENTS

3/4 cup butter, softened

1-3/4 cups sugar

2 eggs

4 cups flour

1 teaspoon baking powder

dash salt

3-4 tablespoons ice water

1 recipe icing (see below)

store-bought decorator's icing with small tip

METHOD

1. Preheat the oven to 400°.

2. In a large mixing bowl, beat the butter until it is smooth and creamy.

3. Add the sugar and mix together.

4. Add the eggs and blend well.

5. In a separate bowl, mix the flour, baking powder, and salt. Gradually add the dry mixture to the wet. Add water as required to hold the dough together.

6. Roll the dough onto a floured board to 1/4"–1/2" thick.

7. With a small knife, cut into postcard-sized rectangles.

8. Place on an ungreased cookie sheet and bake until edges just begin to brown, about 7 minutes.

9. Using a spatula, transfer the rectangles to a rack and let cool. While cooling, prepare icing.

10. With a butter knife or small spatula, fill the background with the icing. Allow to dry.

11. Once the background is set, write your postcards with decorator icing. Add an icing stamp and postmark with decorating icing if you wish.

ICING INGREDIENTS

2 egg whites

3 cups powdered sugar

1 tablespoon lemon juice

1/4 teaspoon salt

METHOD

Combine all the ingredients in a bowl. Mix about 1 minute until well blended.

Use these postcards as hand-delivered invitations to a party, or just to say hello to friends.

Makes 6–8 postcards

MASTER**CHOCOLATECAKE**

INGREDIENTS

3	ounces unsweetened chocolate	1/3	cup vegetable shortening
2	cups flour	1	cup sour cream
1	teaspoon baking soda	2	eggs
1	teaspoon salt	1	teaspoon vanilla extract
1-1/2	cups sugar	1/4	cup hot water

METHOD

1. Preheat the oven to 350°. Grease and flour cake pans or place cupcake liners in muffin tins, depending on what you are going to make.

2. Use a double boiler (or the microwave) to melt the chocolate. The chocolate can also be melted in a small saucepan or metal bowl. To do so, fill a slightly larger saucepan with 2 inches of water and place over low heat. Place the smaller pan or bowl in the larger saucepan and let the chocolate melt. Set aside to cool.

3. In a large mixing bowl, sift together the flour, baking soda, salt, and sugar.

4. Add the shortening and sour cream to the flour mixture and beat well.

5. Stir in the melted chocolate.

6. Add the eggs, one at a time, and beat between each addition.

7. Add the vanilla and hot water, and beat until the batter is smooth.

8. Pour the batter into the cake pans or cupcake liners. If baking in cake pans, bake 25–30 minutes, until a toothpick inserted into the cake comes out clean. If baking cupcakes, bake for 15–18 minutes, until a toothpick inserted into a cupcake comes out clean.

9. Remove from the oven and let cool about 10 minutes, then turn the cakes out of the pans and onto racks to finish cooling completely.

Makes two 8" cake layers or about 24 cupcakes.

MASTER**RECIPES**

MASTER RECIPES

MASTER**YELLOW**CAKE

INGREDIENTS

3 cups cake flour, sifted	1-3/4 cups sugar
2-1/2 teaspoons baking powder	2 eggs
1/2 teaspoon salt	1 teaspoon vanilla extract
2/3 cup unsalted butter, softened	1-1/4 cups whole milk

METHOD

1. Preheat the oven to 350°. Grease and flour cake pans or place cupcake liners in muffin tins, depending on what you are going to make.

2. In a large bowl, sift together the flour, baking powder, and salt.

3. In a separate bowl, cream the butter. Gradually add the sugar, creaming until light and fluffy.

4. Add the eggs one at a time, and beat between each addition.

5. Add the vanilla to the milk.

6. Add about a quarter of the flour mixture and mix well. Add about a quarter of the milk mixture and mix well. Continue alternating flour mixture and milk mixture, beating after each addition until smooth.

7. Pour the batter into the cake pans or cupcake liners. If baking in cake pans, bake for 25–30 minutes, or until a toothpick inserted into the cake comes out clean and the cake is pulling away slightly from the sides of the pan. If baking cupcakes, bake for 15–18 minutes, until a toothpick inserted into a cupcake comes out clean.

8. Remove from the oven and let cool about 10 minutes, then turn the cakes out of the pans and onto racks to finish cooling completely.

Makes two 9" cake layers or about 30 cupcakes

MASTER**BUTTER-CREAM**ICING

INGREDIENTS

1/2 cup butter, softened

4 cups powdered sugar

1/2 teaspoon salt

1/3 cup milk

1 teaspoon vanilla extract

METHOD

1. In a large bowl, cream the butter until smooth.

2. Add the sugar, salt, milk, and vanilla, and mix until smooth and creamy.

3. If desired, add a few drops of food coloring and mix well.

4. Spread onto cake or cupcakes.

Ices one regular-sized cake (two 9" layers) or 24–30 cupcakes

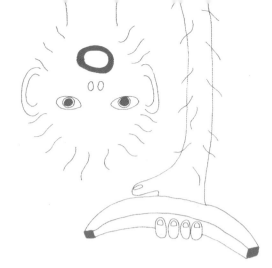

ACKNOWLEDGMENTS

Thanks sooo much for your beautiful and inspired photography, Eric Staudenmaier.

Thanks sooo much for your completely amazing and creative food styling, Lisa Barnett.

Thanks for the use of your beautiful Silver Lake homes, yards, and cars: Eli Bonerz, Samantha Gore, Greg Pestoni, Mike Mills, Melody McDaniel, and John Harris.

Thanks so much for your helping hands: Samantha Gore, Nancy Stiener, Yolanda Yorke-Edgell, April Napier, and Ann Faison.

Thanks so much for your wise advice and terrific ideas: Michael Polish, Phil Morrison, Ann Faison, Roz Music, Jennifer Weisberg, Patrick Nolan, Douglas Gayeton, James Chinlund, Heather Levine, Dee Dee Gordon, Susan Hootstein, Karen Hillenberg, and the New School of Cooking.

Thanks so much for being the most wonderful, smart, and creative editor: Duncan Bock.

Thanks for your guidance and faith: Charlie Melcher and Alessandra Balzer.

Thanks for your love and support: Mom, Daddy, Libby, Paul, and Zep.

Thanks for your great design: Gary Tooth.

This book was produced by Melcher Media, Inc., 124 W. 13th Street, New York, N.Y. 10011.

Publisher: Charles Melcher
Senior Editor: Duncan Bock
Editor: Lia Ronnen
Assistant Editor: Megan Worman
Publishing Manager: Bonnie Eldon
Editorial Assistant: Lauren Nathan
Design: Empire Design Studio, NYC
Production Director: Andrea Hirsh

Special thanks to Lesley Bruynesteyn, Janet Saines, Danielle Svetcov.

Jell-O® is a registered trademark of KF Holdings. Used with permission.

Hostess Sno Balls® is a registered trademark of Interstate Brands Corporation.

Fruit Roll-Ups® is a registered trademark of General Mills, Inc.

Kids should always have an adult's help when creating in the kitchen. Neither the publisher, the producer, nor the author can assume any responsibility for any accident, injuries, losses, or other damages resulting from the use of this book.

First Hyperion Paperback edition, 2005
1 3 5 7 9 10 8 6 4 2

ISBN 0-7868-3735-7 (pbk.)

Library of Congress Cataloging-in-Publication Data is on file.

Printed in China